A catalogue record for this book is available from the British Library
Published by Ladybird Books Ltd
80 Strand London WC2R ORL
A Penguin Company

1 3 5 7 9 10 8 6 4 2

Animal Stories

Roaring Rory

written by Ronne Randall

illustrated by John Haslam

Ladybird

Out on the sunny plain, the Lion family lounged and lazed. Lions love to laze!

Roaring Rory loved lazing more than anyone. He loved to S T R E T C H and feel the warm sun on his back...

and his belly...

Mum and Dad were teaching Rory how to be a big lion. That meant learning to stalk, prowl and pounce.
"Show me what you've learned," said Mum.

Stalk... prowl... POUNCE!

went Rory.

"Perfect!" said Mum.

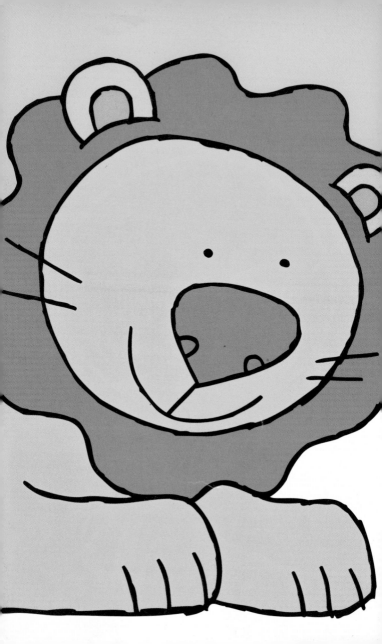

Dad was teaching Rory to growl, rumble and roar.
Rory opened his mouth wide, and gave a mighty R R O W R R !
"Just right!" said Dad. "You'll soon be ready!"

But, although Rory was good at lion lessons, his favourite time was when lessons were over.

Then he could snooze and snore
in the sunshine.

Rory's brothers and sisters always wanted to play.
"Get up!" said his sister. "Let's play Leaping Lions!"
"Not now," said Rory. "I haven't finished napping yet!"

"Rory!" called his brother. "Let's chase butterflies!"
"Not now," said Rory, turning over. "I'm right in the middle of a wonderful dream!"

"What a lazy lion you are!" said Mum.
"When you are a big lion, you will have
to stay awake for much longer."

"Then I want to stay a little lion for ever," said Rory. But he didn't really mean it.

Late one night, Rory woke up suddenly. His nose began to twitch. Something was rustling nearby!

Rory followed his nose into the bush.
He remembered what he'd learned
in lion lessons.
"I can be a big lion if I want to,"
he thought.

He stalked...and prowled...

and he P O U N C E D with a growl
and a

RRROWWWR!

"Boo!" said Rory's little sister. "Ready to play hide and seek?"
"In the morning," yawned Rory. "It's time for sleep."

The next morning, while the other young lions were having lion lessons and playing, Rory had a lie-in.

"Shhh," said Mum and Dad, when the other cubs tried to wake him. "Rory needs his rest. He's a big lion now. A special roaring, prowling night-time lion!"

Rory smiled, sleepily. Not only had he become a big lion, he could still spend all day doing just what he liked best... sleeping in the sun!